A BROWN PAPER **PRE**SCHOOL BOOK

RAZZLE DAZZLE DOODLE **ART**

Creative Play for You and Your Young Child

by Linda Allison and Martha Weston

Little, Brown and Company

Boston   New York   Toronto   London

The authors thank the moms, dads, aunts, uncles, teachers, librarians, and kids who generously shared their ideas, stories, and experience for this book.

A special thanks to Tracy Williams, Ethel Seiderman, and the kids and staff at the Fairfax–San Anselmo Children's Center, Kathy Keswick, and the kids and staff at the San Anselmo Preschool, Betsy Partridge, Ann Pope, Barbara Young, and Joyce Hakansson.

A very special thanks to Patricia Monighan Nourot, Ph.D., Professor of Early Childhood Education at Sonoma State University, for guiding the content and adding her ideas, humor, and expert review.

FIRST EDITION

10 9 8 7 6 5 4 3 2 1

IM

Published simultaneously in Canada by Little, Brown & Company (Canada) Limited

The Brown Paper Preschool books are edited and prepared for publication at The Yolla Bolly Press, Covelo, California, under the supervision of James and Carolyn Robertson. Editorial and production staff: Renee Menge, Diana Fairbanks, and Alexandra Chappell. Composition by Wilsted & Taylor, Oakland.

Library of Congress Cataloging-in-Publication Data

Allison, Linda.
    Razzle dazzle doodle art : creative play for you and your young child / by Linda Allison and Martha Weston. — 1st ed.
       p. cm. — (A Brown paper preschool book)
    ISBN 0-316-03465-7
    1. Art—Study and teaching (Preschool)
2. Education, Preschool—Activity programs.
I. Weston, Martha. II. Title. III. Series.
LB1140.5.A7A45   1991
372.5—dc20   93-24556

Printed in Hong Kong

★ CONTENTS ★

ODDS & ENDS

SKILLS LIST

INDEX

★ ABOUT THIS BOOK ★
ARTFUL LEARNING

Why art? It's so messy. You don't have time. Anyway, you're not artistic. There are a lot of reasons not to do art with your child. On the other hand . . .

Art can boost a kid's self-esteem. If you have ever heard "Look what I made," you know that creating things can make a child feel really powerful.

Art is expressive. It can give your child a language beyond words: "You drew a scary snake." It can also be a vehicle for exploring your child's emotions: "How does that black snake make you feel?"

Art lets a child test cause and effect. "I smashed clay flat. Then I squeezed it, and it squirted out my fingers." Playing with materials and finding out what things will and will not do gives little ones a lab for all sorts of wild experiments.

Art is a challenge. It presents many ways to exercise your child's problem-solving muscles. "How do you draw a fish in a lake?" "How do you stick these together?" Every artist has to push his ingenuity and stretch his imagination and creativity to get results.

Art is a good exercise for building hand strength, finger dexterity, and hand-eye coordination.

Believe it or not, art is academic. It connects to mathematical and spatial thinking in many ways. It is also a language of symbols that can be discussed and understood before your child ventures into the symbols of letters and words.

Art encourages your child to work and play quietly, and it's a great way to share time with your child. Together you can do the dangerous (finger paint with chocolate pudding), the wild (wear sticky notes on your nose), or the seemingly impossible (build a two-foot garbanzo-bean tower). You can give your child the special attention it takes to learn how to tie a knot or make the stapler work.

But most of all, art can be pure sensory fun and exploration for your child, and who knows, maybe even for you.

★ ART SPOT ★

Make an art spot at your house. All you need is a table and a shelf for stashing gear. Or you can create an art box that travels to the kitchen table or wherever the studio will be that day. An old suitcase works great.

Paper. Scrap paper is fine. Use backs of office paper, wallpaper, brown bags, napkins, and paper towels.

Store **buttons, beads,** etc. in glass jars.

Pens & Pencils. Fill a box with all the weird ones that accumulate. (Washable are best.)

Washable Markers. Keep them in a marker minder. The tops are held in place by play dough, plasticine, or plaster of paris in a shoe box lid.

Smock. → Use an apron or old shirt.

White glue and **glue stick**.

Keep **Scissors, string,** and **yarn** in an oatmeal carton.

Crayons. Make a crayon catcher with slits cut in a plastic lid.

Work Area. Cutting, pasting, or painting on a plastic-coated place mat, shallow box, or cookie sheet makes for easy cleanup.

More Paper. Construction paper, old magazines, gift wrap, greeting cards, and junk mail are all good for cutting up. Printers sometimes have scraps for the asking.

Scissors. A good pair of kid scissors is a must. Test them first — if you have a hard time with them, you can be sure your child will. Accommodate your left-handed child with left-handed scissors.

Glue. The easiest glue for little ones to use is a glue stick. A small squeeze bottle of white glue works well for little hands. Save money by buying a big bottle to refill the small one when it runs low.

Cleanup is the hard part of projects for the adult helper. But for a preschooler, sorting colored crayons into cans, wiping a table, or peeling up tape can be fun, especially if you make it a game.

"OK, Chris, can you pick up all the pink dots off the floor? I'll do the others." "Jana, let's put all the crayons back in their house. I think their mother is calling them."

Calling out colors or shapes, making it a race, or telling a story about sorting are all ways to make cleanup extra fun.

See how many markers you can put away before the bell rings!

TIC TIC TIC TIC

★ EVOLVING ART ★

Visual art appears to be a universal language. Children from around the world may draw different things, but how their drawing skills develop is amazingly similar. Children have their own personal timetables, but the sequence is much the same.

Watch how children's art changes and grows, and you will get a fascinating glimpse at how their thinking and coordination skills are growing and changing.

Scribbles. Kids pick up crayons at a very early age for the pure tactile enjoyment of making marks. In the earliest stages, they are learning how to hold crayons, to scribble, and to experiment. Baby artists love to taste the tools.

Controlled Scribbles. Next, scribbles begin to have a real direction and a pattern as children learn how to make lines. Kids start by forming shapes such as circles, then try more complex shapes such as triangles and boxes.

Drawing and Naming. Soon, their marks begin to take on meaning. Circles become eyes, and squares mean houses. Their work shows increasing control and a whole vocabulary of shapes. Lines begin to stand for things. "This is a snake." "This is my mom." Kids at this stage usually draw first, then name things that they see in their work.

"A dinosaur. My dinosaur is not sick. Chicken and bones and dots."

"A dinosaur with a tail. A zebra. A zoo! Lots of animals."

"That's a lion and he doesn't roar because he's just a picture."

Representational Art. At this stage, children generally have an idea in mind before they start to draw. Their drawings become more about making ideas appear on paper. These drawings show details that mimic real life, such as a person's hair color or the number of brothers and sisters in a family. Most kids reach this stage by kindergarten, but many arrive sooner.

"Elephant"

"A scary monster"

"Mommy"

"Daddy"

"Me"

Don't try and hurry your child. No stage is better than another. Sit back and enjoy the spectacle of watching your child's skills and awareness of the world unfold. Add captions or titles when your child describes his drawing.

★ DRAWING GAMES ★

If your little one doesn't grab a pencil and immediately start filling the page with big, bold strokes, don't be disappointed. Kids can be shy about drawing. Break the ice by drawing many different ways. Most of all, don't forget to have fun.

Copycat Drawing. "Can you make a line like this? A zigzag line? Loops? Teeny loops? Draw with your whole arm? With just your fingers?" Invite your child to make the first marks; then you copy. Do it wrong. Kids love to point out your mistakes.

Connect the Dots. Dab the paper with random dots (or sticky dots). Connect the dots with a straight line of another color. What do you see?

Double Draw. Tape down a big piece of paper. Grab a marker in each hand. Draw with both hands at once. Can you make each drawing the same? Different?

Trace. Put your child's hand down and trace around it to make an outline. Let your child try tracing your hand. Trace around a can or a doll. Some kids adore tracing anything that will hold still.

★ STICKER WHISKERS & FUNNY FACES ★

They're bright, they're sticky, they peel, and they're fun to feel. Whatever it is, there is something about stickers that little kids love. Even the tiniest kids can use them to make faces. Here's how.

You will need:

paper
markers
scissors
sticky dots (any round stickers)
sticky notes

1. "Kathy, do you want to make faces? Let's draw a circle to start."
2. "Here are two eyes." (Show the dots.) "I'm gonna stick one eye here. Where should the other one go? Maybe you'd like to stick it on."
3. "Here's a nose, but where should it go?"
4. "Want to draw in the mouth?"
5. "Add some whiskers?"
6. "Want to try one by yourself?"

Drawing Circles

Little ones have trouble drawing circles. Why not make circles by holding the marker together until your child gets the feel of how it's done? (Remember how much fun it was learning to dance by standing on your dad's feet?)

"Guy with 3 eyes."

Why's that on your nose?

For fun. Want one?

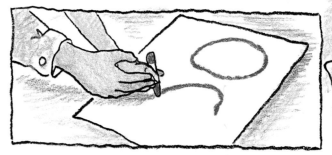

★ DRAWING BIG TIME ★

Paper? Pencil? Phooey! Stick a finger in the sandbox or drag a stick across the mud at the beach. Get loose; get crazy. Try these wacky ways to draw.

Glass Wax. Turn a glass door into a giant drawing pad. All you need is a coat of glass cleaner that turns windows white. Let your kid spread it on. Then have him use his finger as a pencil. It's easy to erase and start again. When he's done, erase all the wax with a soft cloth—clean windows and art at the same time!

Sidewalk Drawing. Make drawings as big as a parking lot! Find a smooth stretch of pavement. Give it a clean sweep.

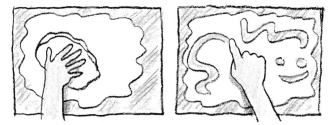

Use big, fat sidewalk chalks. (Skinny kinds don't live long on the street.) Draw big and bold. Get crazy and have fun. Leave the art for others to discover.

Ice Art. A cool way to draw on a hot day. All you need are some ice cubes and a smooth piece of sidewalk. On really hot days, draw fast, before the lines disappear. This technique is good for big, loose, easy-come, easy-go art.

FROZEN PENCIL

Freeze water in a juice can.

Peel paper and draw.

The dragon's head is gone!

I'll fix it!

CRAYON CUPCAKES

All too soon those boxes of nice new crayons turn into heaps of stubby wax bits. Instead of throwing them out, gather them together and melt them into big, fat, multicolored crayon cupcakes. Make them dark or light, or mix the colors up. It's easy:

325°
2 minutes

Peel off the papers (your child can help here). Put a handful of crayons in a cupcake tin. Bake at 325°F until the crayons soften (about two minutes). Let the cupcakes cool, then pop them out of the tin. Draw!

★ MAZES & DOTS ★

Here are two drawing games for those must-be-quiet times. Even if your child doesn't quite understand the rules, he can play along and enjoy a quiet moment with the pleasure of all your attention.

Mazes can keep some kids glued to their seats for an astounding amount of time. Start easy, but don't be surprised if you must quickly begin adding loops and dead ends to keep your young one challenged.

1. Draw a simple curved pathway with a clear start and finish.

Hints: Don't be too quick to help. Puzzling exercises your kid's problem-solving muscles. Color the path and add more stickers for fun. Some kids tell amazing stories about where they've been.

2. A theme makes this game more exciting. "Hey, Anna, who do you want to take on a trip? Pick a sticker. Where do you want it to go? The moon?" Mark the destination with an X.

3. "Ready? Start here and draw your way down the road to the X. No fair crossing a line."

Dots. To play this game, your child needs to be able to draw a straight line and take turns. (If not, it's good practice, but expect a more free-form result.)

1. Set up a small grid pattern of dots.

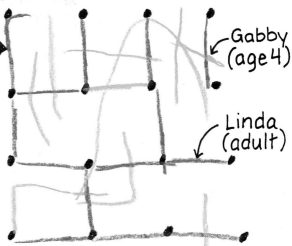

Gabby (age 4)

Linda (adult)

For Fun: Increase the size of the grid for a harder game. Kids may enjoy counting their boxes. With experience, older children will begin to anticipate the geometry of this game and will form a strategy to make the most boxes. Play dumb so your kid can win.

2. Watch: I go first with the red marker. I draw a line from dot to dot.

(Connect two neighbor dots only—no diagonals, skips, or curves allowed.)

3. Your turn.

I'm blue.

4. Look! You made a box! Put your letter in it. Now take an extra turn.

"S" for Sara.

My turn dot to dot! Look, I made a house!

It's a maze!

Okay, Terra, put your letter inside the house.

★ NEON CHALK ★

Draw big and bright! Yogurt has the magic quality of softening chalk so it goes on thick and smooth; plus it acts as a fixer so the chalk won't smear once it dries. Team chalk with brown bags for low-cost, high-contrast art.

These guys are going to get smooshed.

I'm putting a white blanket on all the people.

You will need:
¼ cup buttermilk or yogurt
water
mint or vanilla flavoring
colored chalk
paper: brown grocery bags, brown wrapping
    paper, or sheets of dark construction paper
shallow bowl
wide paintbrush

Dip and Draw. Pour ½ inch of fixer into the shallow bowl. Wet the end of the chalk in the fixer, and draw.

Draw and Paint. Make a chalk drawing. Paint on a coat of fixer with a wide brush. Be careful. Pushing too hard with the brush makes the color disappear.

Fixer. Thin the yogurt or buttermilk until it is the consistency of cream. Add a few drops of the mint or vanilla flavoring for a nice scent.

Give Your Child Time to try out a new activity in her own way. Sometimes it helps to offer a starting place. Try drawing on big paper, using big strokes. If you make it look like fun, your child will want to join you. You can draw a geometric design and color it together, using big, loose, scribbly strokes.

★ ART-TO-GO KIT ★

Ten minutes can be an eternity if you have to spend it with a fidgety preschooler in a waiting room. Turn those terrible eternities into pleasant intermissions. Just pack an art-to-go kit.

These purple stars are all friends. I need more on my boat.

You will need:
Ziploc bag
paper tablet (with a hard back)
pencils
markers (washable)
crayons
stickers (any kind)

Stickers. Packs of inexpensive stickers can be purchased at the supermarket. Younger kids enjoy just making them stick. Older kids like to use them as characters in their drawings. Try them as a starting place for a sticker story. "Once there was a red dot lost in the mountains. All the dot could see was the stars. . . ."

Zachary rushes in with his latest creation, and you say, "What is it?" It's a natural response, but not really a helpful one for a couple of reasons.

There is a good chance Zachary doesn't know what it is. Little kids like to experiment with art materials for pure sensory pleasure. Often they can't name their artwork. "What is it?" implies that their work *needs* to be something.

"What is it?" also invites a one-word answer. To encourage your kid's verbal skills, invite him to talk with a question like "Tell me about your work" or "Wow, how did you do that?"

Sometimes it's hard not to respond to your child's picture with a "What a nice dog!" or "What a pretty flower!" By emphasizing "nice" and "pretty," you set your kid up to draw hearts, flowers, and happy faces. Just describe what you see. "What energetic lines. Wow, what wild colors. Look at those wiggles." Your kid wants your feedback and attention, but you don't have to love every creation in order to be an enthusiastic supporter.

It's even better to describe what you see in ways that sharpen your child's perceptions. Try out words such as *bright*, *enormous*, *soft*, *vivid*, *fat*, *thin*, *zigzag*, or *wavy*. This kind of conversation helps your kid to observe and appreciate what he has done and expands his vocabulary at the same time.

★ WILD-AND-CRAZY PAINT ★

There are many ways to paint. Some of them don't need a brush. Heck, for some, you don't even need paint. Have fun exploring them all.

Painting Big Time. Little ones love to paint, even with just water. On a warm day, give them a fat painter's brush and a bucket of water. Turn them loose outside to "paint" the house or the driveway.

water

Sponge Painting. Cut kitchen sponges into simple shapes. Dip them in paint and press them onto paper.

Newspaper Painting. Tape sheets of newspaper onto the table. Set up tempera and a large brush. Tell your child to paint around all the people in the pictures. The paper is really cheap, and the results are interesting.

Marble Painting. Place several pieces of paper on a cookie sheet. Pour a small amount of tempera into a shallow plastic dish. Roll a marble around in the paint. Carefully place the marble on the paper, and roll it around to make it "paint." It's more fun with a couple of colored marbles (or even a golf ball).

marble

paint
paper
cookie
sheet

TA-DA!

★ PAINT SETUP ★

Sometimes even artist moms and designer dads skip painting with their preschoolers because it is too messy. That's a pity. Exploring with paint is a real thrill for little ones. The trick is to minimize the mess and maximize the fun.

Kid Cover. Wear old clothes or one of Dad's old shirts. If it's warm, wear nothing at all!

Painters. Big fat brushes work best for small hands. (Get cheap ones from paint stores, especially those foam wedges.) Also try straws, sticks, feathers, rollers, toothbrushes, cotton swabs, forks, sponges, or squeegees.

Use a **Big Jar** of **Water** for cleaning the brushes.

Containers. Use small amounts of washable paint in wide-mouth jars. A muffin tin works well too. Add a **Sponge** collar to handle the paint dribbles.

A **Cheap Drop Cloth** or old shower curtain will minimize cleanup.

Easy Easel. The corner of a large cardboard box can be cut away to make an easel. Tape or clip the paper in place.

①

Cut.

Cut.

② Score.

Cut a slit for a clip.

③ Fold in.

④ Fold in.

Fold up.

⑤ Turn over.

Tape.

This is the bottom

Paint. Make sure it is nontoxic and washable. Tempera is the classic kid paint. The powder form is cheapest, but the premixed is easiest. Here are some interesting additions, whichever kind you use:

- A squirt of liquid detergent prevents cracking, eases cleanup, and makes paint adhere to slick surfaces.

- A few drops of oil of wintergreen keep paint fresh longer.

- Food flavoring (mint or cherry) adds an interesting dimension of smell.

- Liquid laundry starch makes paint creamy and adds a gloss.

- Salt adds sparkle and body to paint.

Watercolors. These paints come in a neat box and are handy for trips. It may take a while for young ones to catch on to using watercolors. When the colors get muddy, a quick rinse under the faucet cleans them right up.

Move Outside. In warm weather, tape paper up on a wall or a fence, or plunk down in an empty wading pool.

Introduce Your Child to New Tools or materials by sitting down to talk about the very basics. "Here's how to hold the brush. Clean it in water this way." Don't forget to mention what not to do: "Don't grind the brush into the paper, because it breaks the bristles."

The brush always gets a bath before it touches the next color.

Cleanup. Taking paint off a table with a soapy sponge is as much fun for a preschooler as putting it on. Of course, having your child help with cleanup takes twice as long, but the lessons learned are worth the investment.

★ SQUIRT PAINTING ★

Squishy fun with a surprise ending—what could be better? Kids of all ages love to squirt paint, but it's especially fun for preschoolers because everybody, no matter what their ability, gets fanciful results.

You will need:
thirsty paper such as newsprint
thick tempera (two or three colors)
plastic squeeze bottles (with small openings)

1. Pour each color into a separate bottle.
2. Cover the table with paper or plastic. Set out the paint and paper.
3. Fold the paper in half, then unfold it.
4. Squirt dabs of paint onto one half of the paper.
5. Fold the paper in half again. Press the paper to smear the paint. "What do you think happened?"
6. Open the paper. "What do you see?"
7. Set it aside to dry. Try another.

Hints: Easy on the paint (too much will squirt out the edges). You'll get better results if you hold the edges while your kid rubs. Naming the resulting shapes and forms is a fun game all by itself.

Squirt Paint. This recipe makes a thick, sparkly paint that really stretches your tempera supply. Mix equal parts of flour, salt, and water in a blender. Blend in enough wet or dry tempera to make a bright color. The results should be about as thick as ketchup.

BUTTERFLIERS

Turn those squirt paintings into a flock of high-flying butterfliers.

You will need:
squirt paintings
scissors
soda straws
tape

You may have to be in charge of the cutting while your child colors and assembles.

1. Cut the squirt art into a butterfly shape.
2. Clip three or four straws at each end.
3. Poke one straw into the end of another until it is tight. Slide all the straws together.
4. Slip the folded part of the paper butterfly into the end of the straw so it's snug. Tape into place.

5. Fly it around the room. (Make a bunch of them to stand in a vase.)

Butterflies from Cards

Pretty butterflies can also be cut from 4 × 6–inch cards. Cut them out, then let your child color them. Mount them on straws.

★ FINGER PAINT ★

No parents in their right mind want the mess of finger paint. Unless they love the pleasure of watching their kid paint with her whole body, experimenting with colors, lines and squiggles to a chorus of giggles. Go ahead, take a chance. Some things are worth the mess.

Finger paint kits can be purchased anywhere that sells toys. A cheaper alternative is to make your own. You'll need:

½ cup cornstarch
4 cups cold water
tempera

Combine cornstarch and water in a saucepan, and stir out the lumps. Stir constantly at a slow boil over low heat until it thickens. Divide the goo into several containers. Stir in washable tempera to make bright colors. A few drops of flavoring, such as mint or cherry, add a delightful smell. It's fun to use this paint when it's still warm.

you have a design you like, make a print by gently pressing a sheet of paper onto the paint. Carefully pull it away. "Wow, look what happened!"

Finger Paint Classic. Finger paint on a sheet of damp paper. Hang the painting out to dry.

Tabletop Prints. Get wild. Paint directly onto a smooth washable tabletop. For a neater approach, paint on a tray or cookie sheet. When

Shaving cream makes a scented, easy-to-clean (but non-saveable) finger paint.

★ BATHTUB BODY PAINT ★

If you can't face the mess of finger paint, try turning liquid soap into finger paint for the bathtub. This paint gets your kid clean with an excursion into art at the same time. It's easy to do and cheap to make.

You will need:
opaque white liquid soap, such as Ivory
containers (squeezable plastic bottles with small openings are best)
food coloring

1. Pour about ½ cup of liquid soap into a squeeze bottle.
2. Add about six drops of food coloring. Shake to mix. Keep adding coloring until you get a bright color.
3. Mix several different colors.

Run a bath. Invite your child to draw on the tub or shower walls or all over himself. Paint right out of the bottle, or smear paint on with the fingers.

Look, Kitty, green blood! Want some??

Meow?

Washable Studio. Some parents say the bathtub makes a fine place to paint. Tape the paper to the wall. Go crazy with paint. Afterward, the artist and the studio can be sudsed up and washed down at once.

★ PICKING APPROPRIATE PROJECTS ★

Choose projects that allow your kid to be the artist, without much help from you (you already know how to cut and paste). You'll know quickly if a project is beyond your kid's abilities, because frustration strikes fast.

> Unco Dan, dees don't cut! I hate dees dum dum scissors!

> That's okay. Let's try tearing the paper instead — maybe into little bits.

Don't Panic. First, try to modify an activity. For instance, if your kid is having a hard time with scissors, try tearing instead. No success? Choose a simpler activity.

Try Again Later. You'll be amazed at how fast a kid's skill level changes. A project that's a miserable flop today can be a big hit in a few weeks.

Be Flexible. You have a great hat project in mind, when suddenly Suzie becomes obsessed with tape. Nothing will distract her. Remember, for three-year-old Suzie, tape is just as interesting and valid as hats. Figure out a way to let her play with tape. Save hats for another day.

Hands Off. You might be tempted to put a finishing touch on a collage or to draw in a mouth, especially if you have artistic tendencies. Override your urge to create a result. Remember that the value of art for young children is in the discovery, not the result.

Show Respect. Value those colorful smears and scribbles and those odd collage constructions. Display your child's art in a proud place. Get your child to sign the art (if she can't write, make sure you do it). These are all ways of telling your kid that her efforts are interesting and worthwhile.

★ CUTTING UP ★

Preschoolers are happy to sit and snip (or attempt to snip) paper for the pure pleasure of making the scissors go. Give them an old magazine, and they can entertain themselves for a good long while.

Magazines and Junk Mail. These are good for cutting up. Make it clear to your child that she needs to get permission before she cuts into anything.

I want to cut out this doggie.

Has anyone seen the electricity bill?

Let's cut!

I made tickets for the movies.

Learning to cut is tough. (If you have forgotten, try cutting with your opposite hand.) There's a lot to it. You have to coordinate your eyes and your hand, finger, and arm muscles, all while holding the scissors at just the right angle (and that is just the cutting hand). It takes strength and practice. You certainly have to admire little ones for being so willing to try. Cutting play clay is good practice for getting the hang of scissors.

Hint: Read about scissors on page 7.

Fancy Cuts. After you child learns scissor control, she will be delighted to learn some scissor tricks. Show her how to cut fringe, how to fold and cut a hole, and how to cut two pieces of paper at once.

Look, I made eyes!

★ STICKY BITS ★

After a holiday or a birthday party, gather up all those bits of brightly colored tissue paper. Flatten them, then stash them. They will be ready to go when you're in the mood to make a colorful sticky bits collage.

You will need:
big sheets of white paper
white glue or liquid starch
tissue paper (bright colors)

1. Assemble a multicolored pile of tissue paper scraps. Cut or tear them into strips and bits. Your child will enjoy this. In fact, you can make it a separate project.

2. Explore. "What colors do you like? What looks good together? How does it look if you put a long skinny strip here?"
3. Paint a sheet of the white paper with a coat of glue. (Dilute it so it brushes on easily.)

4. Apply the tissue to the sticky surface. "What happens when you put color over color?"
5. Another coat of glue makes the tissue colors melt and run. Let it dry.

Hints: Foil paper, strips of ribbon, stars, and seals are great for jazzing up a tissue paper collage. Try working on a sheet of aluminum foil for a silvery background.

Ooohhh, glue! Little kids love glue. It follows the unwritten kid law: If it's messy, kids will love it. Here are some ways to cope with glue:

- Use a small amount in a lid with a cotton swab or a stick

- Use small squeeze bottles and clean them at the end of a session

- Use glue sticks

Glitter Paint. Sparkles are always a hit with little kids. Draw lines on paper with squeeze bottles of white glue. Sprinkle glitter on the lines while the glue is still wet. Shake the excess glitter onto a paper and return it to the bottle. Cornmeal or colored sand can also be used.

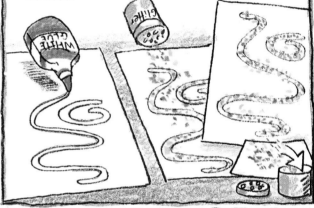

Glow Glue. White glue takes on a whole new personality if you add a squeeze of food coloring. Shake it to make a bright color. It goes on like glue, but it looks like paint. Great for collages.

★ FOUND FACES ★

Play this art game with sticks and stones on the sidewalk, with shells on the beach, or with household stuff on paper. It's fun to make faces with whatever you find. Junk art, or found faces, is a great way to invite your imagination out to play.

You will need:
sheet of paper
scissors
found items such as bottle caps, feathers,
    stones, coins, marbles, or any small odds and
    ends

1. Set out the paper. Put down the scissors in the center. "Do you see anybody?"
2. Add some eyes. "See anybody now?"

3. Draw a mouth or add an item. "Now who is there? Is he happy or sad?"
4. "Let's take him apart and make another."

CLOUDS AND CRACKS
Sit back and watch the clouds roll by with your child. What do you see? Dogs? Hogs? Or nothing at all? Leonardo da Vinci, the great Renaissance artist, described lying in bed and finding faces in the cracks of his plaster walls. Centuries later, the same game works well with cracks, clouds, doorknobs that look like noses, or headlights that look like eyes.

★ YIPES, STRIPES! ★

Tunnels, roller coasters, or wiggle worms—kids call these 3-D inventions by all sorts of names. This project takes a minimum of fuss, and kids of all ages will enjoy giving it a try. Bright contrasting colors make the liveliest results.

I need more tape!

Try knots, rings, and loop-the-loop variations.

You will need:
old magazines, construction paper, or gift wrap
sheets of heavy paper
tape or sticky dots

1. Cut paper strips in a variety of widths and lengths.
2. Set out the materials. Show your kid how to attach the tape (or sticky dots) to each end of a paper strip. Stick the strip ends to a sheet of heavy paper, making a tunnel.
3. Let your kid try. Add more strips—until it feels done.

TAPE
It's a rare preschooler who has the finger dexterity and strength to master the tape dispenser. Cut a number of tape pieces and stick them along the edge of a table so they are ready to go. Or try using sticky dots instead.

★ **LEARNING STYLES** ★

If you hang out at your kid's preschool, you will be amazed at how very different these tiny children are. Something as simple as clay will get a whole range of responses. One kid will be attracted to the color, another the smell, and another will punch and pound a lump of clay with his whole body. One child will spend a long time creating a tiny clay fantasy world and tell you a story about it, while her friend will have wandered off bored, in search of puzzles.

Research in education is turning up evidence to support what insightful parents and teachers have known for a long time: there are many ways to be smart. Unfortunately, our school system emphasizes and rewards math and language skills more than other, less quantifiable skills.

One model of human intelligence, developed by psychologist Howard Gardener, describes seven kinds of intelligence. He believes all people have abilities in each area but are naturally stronger in some areas. Here are the seven kinds of intelligence:

Logical-Mathematical: loves puzzles, strategy games, testing, computers, reasoning things out

Musical: sings songs, remembers tunes, mimics noises, plays music

Kinesthetic: athletic, loves to move, likes touching things and people

Linguistic: enjoys words, stories, and writing

Spatial: visual, draws, thinks in pictures, daydreams, enjoys mazes and maps

Interpersonal: socially smart, enjoys friends and groups

Intrapersonal: independent, strong willed, likes pursuing projects alone, reflects on own thinking

Everyone has his own particular learning style based on his particular set of smarts. One is not better than another. Each needs to be honored and nurtured in its own way. A musical child learns to count most easily with a song. So why not sing along and enjoy the music?

★ BONZO BEAN BUILDING ★

A nifty, nontoxic building kit can be found in your kitchen cupboard. Any kid who can handle a toothpick safely can do this project. Children with a flair for building can stick together some pretty elaborate creations.

You will need:
garbanzo beans (canned or cooked)
toothpicks

1. Rinse the beans.
2. Set out a supply of toothpicks and beans. Work on a tray or a cookie sheet.
3. Begin sticking toothpicks and beans together.
4. Add on and on until it feels finished.

5. Set the toothpick creation aside to dry for a day or two. The beans harden up and set the toothpicks in place.

Animals, people, houses, and geometrics are possible. First, let your builder explore. Later you might show your child how to make something stand up or how to make an animal. Give the creation a name.

★ PLAY CLAY ★

Poke a hole and squish it up. Make a snake and smash it flat. Clay lets kids experiment with cause and effect by building and breaking. It strengthens hand and finger muscles. Clay play is packed with all sorts of powerful lessons.

The Best Clay. Find the kind that stays soft, allowing kids to work the clay to their heart's content, day after day. Play-Doh can be purchased at any toy store in a variety of bright colors. A safe, cheap, homemade version is easy to cook up. Maybe your kid would like to help?

STAY-SOFT PLAY CLAY

2 Tbsp. oil
1 cup flour
½ cup salt
2 tsp. cream of tartar
1 cup water
wax paper
food coloring
food flavoring (for scent)

Warm the oil in a saucepan. Stir in the flour, salt, cream of tartar, and water. Cook for three minutes, stirring constantly. Drop the dough onto wax paper. Knead in drops of food coloring until you get a bright color. Add a drop or two of flavoring if you like.

Keep the dough soft by storing it in a sealed bag or container. It has a shelf life of at least six weeks if it's kept in the fridge.

Pokers and Rollers. A lump of clay and a few household items are enough to keep little ones busy. Kids may need some start-up help to make a ball and roll it flat. Then spoons, forks, string, paper clips, pencils, straws, or cookie cutters can be used to leave interesting impressions.

Clay and Tiny Toys. This combination invites pretend play. Many children build entire fantasy worlds for their small pals. "Rosie, do you think your dinosaur would like a house?" Get ready to participate in a game of pretend. "Mom, taste my green pies."

Watch, Casey. I'll show you how to make a snake.

Cut Clay. Kid scissors work great on play clay. It's a great way for kids to get the feel of cutting.

Molders. Press clay into a "mold" such as a tablespoon and peel it out. Older kids like making shapes this way. Try tiny measuring cups, caps, or molds.

Take It Out on Play Clay. A perfectly acceptable way for your child to act out his fury and aggression is to pound, poke, and pinch clay. "Russell, it's not OK to hit Anna. If you need to hit something, pound this ball of clay."

★ SUPER-DUPER COLOR COOKIES ★

Use this cookie dough as you would play clay, except you can bake and eat the results. Kids of all ages love making these cookies. It's hard to make a bad-looking cookie with this bright-colored dough.

Oohh! I'm squishing all the colors!

Hints:
- It's best to work with chilled dough because it becomes stickier as it warms up.
- Bake similar-size cookies on the same sheet. Cut the really big cookies into wedges.
- Scrape the table with a spatula to pick up bits. Ball them up into multi-colored cookies.
- Make a roll. Slice it into disks. Add a color dot.

SUPER-DUPER DOUGH
2 sticks butter
½ cup sugar
2 eggs
2½ cups flour
2 tsp. baking powder
1 tsp. food flavoring
food coloring
wax paper

1. Blend all the ingredients (except the food coloring) to make a smooth, stiff dough.
2. Divide the dough into two to four sections.
3. Blend in enough food coloring to make each section of dough really bright.
4. Wrap the dough in wax paper. Refrigerate. Makes about 2 cups.
5. Model the chilled dough like play clay. Put cookie sculptures on an oiled baking sheet. Bake 7 to 12 minutes at 375°F.

Sometimes It's Hard to let kids poke and squeeze when you know they will end up making brown muck out of all those great colors. Generally, it's best to get out of the way. Let your kid explore. (If you want perfect results, make your own cookies.)

★ TALL TOWERS ★

Boys and girls love the excitement of building big. But not as much as they love the big crash that always follows. This is a good project for a group if the architects can agree on a demolition time.

Bag #1, stuffed with newspaper wads

Bag #2 fits over #1 and is taped on.

Yoo hoo! Come find me!

Look how tall!

What do you call these I'm making?

Hint: When you get tired of tripping over the blocks, simply break them down and bag them up for the recycler.

Brown Bag Blocks. Stuff a grocery bag with wadded-up newspapers. Slide another bag over the open end. Tape it to make a sturdy closure. Make a pile of them. Your child will enjoy helping with the stuffing part.

Things to Build

- How high a tower can you make? (Count the blocks.)

- Build a fort. Can you get inside?

- Make a tunnel. Can you crawl under?

- Stack up a fence. Keep out.

- Make a hiding place.

FOAM BLOCKS

Styrofoam packing shapes make strong, lightweight building blocks. Save your own. Plus furniture, office equipment, or car stereo stores, and recyclers collect Styrofoam chunks. They might be happy to pass some on to you.

I'm in the middle!

★ ART TOGETHER ★

Sometimes your child will ask you to do the art. She will want to sit back and watch you draw or paint something.

There are many reasons to go along with the game. Sometimes your kid will run out of ideas. She might just want something to color—she doesn't know how to make a bike, and she wants to see how you do it. As long as you don't make a habit of taking over for your child, it's fine to let her be the art director.

"Draw a house for me, Mom."
"OK. What color?"
"Should I make the roof purple too? There, what else does it need?"
"How about a door? Where should it go? Show me."
"Uh-oh, how will we get in? Better draw a door handle. You draw it in."
"Windows? How many? OK, six. Is that enough? Let's count."

Make the process a conversation. Count the windows. Let your child show you where the trees should go. "Are there flowers in the yard?"

Imagine more. "Who do you think lives in the house? Do they have any pets?" Making art tends to open up a child's conversation in interesting ways. Kids who don't have much to say will sometimes make up elaborate tales about a drawing or a clay world they are building. Listen to those tales. They contain the ideas, characters, hopes, and fears that color your child's world.

Write the story on the picture as your child talks. Kids love seeing their ideas translated into letters and words. The process is magical, especially when you read the caption to them later. It's a wonderful way to record the moment in symbols, symbols that show the power and pleasure of reading. Meanwhile, grab your crayons. "Now, Alex, are you ready to color that house?"

★ HOLEY POKE CARDS ★

For little ones who love exploring the ins and outs of holes, these cards are perfect. Lace them with crazy colors and beads. Hang them up or wear them around your neck. Unlace them for another day. They're great on a trip.

You will need:

shoe box scraps or poster board
colorful yarn, string, or shoelaces
beads, pasta, or card bits
paper punch

1. Cut 3 × 5–inch cards from the box scraps or poster board.
2. Punch each card with random holes.
3. Cut 12- to 15-inch lengths of string or yarn.
4. Tape or tie one end of the string to the card. Invite your child to lace the string in and out of the holes.
5. For extra texture, string on beads or paper bits that have been punched with holes.

First-timers might need some start-up help.

First you poke the string into a hole. Now you pull. Find another hole and poke it through. Pull.. Poke... Pull .. . Poke.

Let me try the punch.

It's too hard!

Mommy, can you tie this?

pasta

large beads

cardboard bits with holes

★ PAPER CLIP CHAINS ★

Between the ages of three and four, most kids magically develop enough finger power to link paper clips. Less dexterous hands are glad to scoop and push a pile of paper clips around a table. Clips are also fun to count and sort by color.

You will need:
paper clips (multicolored ones look best)

1. Pour out a pile of clips. Let your kid explore them.
2. Show her how to link the clips. "Look, Christine, slide the loops together and pull. Want to try?" Leave your child to experiment on her own.
3. Trouble? You link, then let your kid pull the links tight.
4. When making a bracelet, you will need to make the last link. "Anna, how many more do you think you need to go around your wrist? Take a guess."

The Junk Necklace is a big hit with preschoolers. Use little plastic toys (the kind your kid collects as party favors). Tiny trucks, plastic superheroes, whistles, and gizmos can all be clipped onto a paper clip necklace.

Hint: An ice pick that's been heated over a hot flame makes a neat hole in soft plastics.

Cool Jewels. Add sticky dots to make some really colorful paper clip jewels. A package of multicolored dots from the stationery store is all you need. The possibilities are limitless. Younger kids like to stick the dots directly onto ribbon. Here are some ideas invented by a gaggle of giggling three-, four-, and five-year-olds:

Toni's clips

ribbon

Stick two dots back to back.

Paula's sticker bracelet

Nick's power bracelet

Learning Colors. There is no need to make a special project of learning colors since children generally learn them at a young age by osmosis. Just pointing them out in everyday work and play is enough. For instance, sorting items into color groups is a good hands-on lesson in sorting and classifying, as well as color names. Bright-colored paper clips are an enjoyable item for a sorting game.

How about those big ones?

These are green. They go here.

Color-Blind. Did you know that one in every 12 boys is color-blind? (And one in every 200 girls?) These kids generally learn to cope with the fact that many colors are hard to differentiate. Some purples can look like blue, greens often appear brown, and a light pink looks gray or even white to their eyes. What's amazing is that the rest of us make the assumption that everyone sees the world the same. It's just not so.

★ REMARKABLE RUBBINGS ★

Even kids who can't draw more than a scribble can make a rubbing (with a little help). As they rub, whatever is underneath the paper appears in all its bumpy detail . . . like magic. Talk about textures that are smooth, nubbly, or scratchy.

You will need:

things to rub (anything flat with a texture or distinctive shape, such as coins, washers, rickrack, rubber bands, string, paper clips, keys, lace, paper doilies, confetti, leaves, or cutouts)

paper (such as newsprint)

tape

crayons

1. Work on a smooth, hard surface. Spread out a handful of things to rub.
2. Cover them with a sheet of paper. Tape the edges down securely so the paper is tight.
3. Rub all over the paper with the side of a crayon.
4. Remove the paper.
5. Rearrange the items. Make another rubbing.

Hints: Young kids need help to keep the paper from slipping. Stickers or paper cutouts are fun to rub.

I made the man.

Look what's there. I pulled it out.

Secret Rubbings. A fun way to introduce this project is to set up a rubbing while your kid isn't looking. Invite your child to touch the paper with her fingertips. "Can you guess what's underneath? No fair peeking. Want to try rubbing it with a crayon? Now what do you see?"

Talk About Art. Whether it's your child's own art or a picture in a book, talking about art can be fun and inventive. Ask your child what he sees.
- "What's the most interesting thing?"
- "Where does your eye go first?"
- "Which color is 'the boss' of the picture?"
- "Is there a story? Can you tell it?"
- "Do you like it? Why? Why not?"
- "What kind of lines does it have? Wiggly? Fat? Skinny? Silly?"

Extend your art talks to whatever you come across—sculptures in the park, stamps at the post office, or a painting in a waiting room. P.S. Don't forget to say what *you* think.

★ SHOWING OFF ART ★

Put it up. Show it off. Celebrate your child's art. The sheer exuberance of kid art can cheer the dingiest of rooms. But more important, displaying your child's artwork sends the message that creative efforts are valued.

The Fridge. This is a perfect space to hang kid art. Magnets are an easy way to hold up art for a temporary show. Rotate works often. Kid artists tend to be very prolific.

Line Up. Pin your kid's art to a clothesline. Strung across the room, it's a fine place to hang your kid's favorites.

The File. At the Weston house, Dad is in charge of the kid art collection. He keeps a file of the kids' best work (he throws away everything but the most adorable). The art has a signature, a date, and often kid comments. Extra-fat files get edited at the end of the year (Dad says the review process is great fun).

Stuffed Drawings. Big artwork can be stuffed for a three-dimensional display. Cut out the picture, leaving a 1-inch margin all around. Cut a backing sheet exactly the same shape. Staple the front and back together at 1-inch intervals along the edge. Leave an opening so you can stuff the creation with crumpled newsprint. Finish stapling. Hang.

Laundry Gallery. The utility room, laundry room, or hall is often a dull spot that can use a gallery of colorful work. A rectangle made from string is an easy way to define the art space.

· FRAME IT ·

IDEA 1

Cut a window.

Tape the picture to cardboard.

Stick tape to inside top edges of both cardboard sheets.

IDEA 2

Cut corners. Tape them for a 3-D look.

★ SKILLS LIST ★

With every activity preschoolers are busy forging basic understandings about how the world works. Basic skills and concepts show up in the range of your child's activities, whether it's painting, sorting bottle caps, or making mud pies. This is a short glossary of the skills and concepts that appear at the bottom of every activity page in this book.

Cause and Effect: Learning to test actions and their results. "I licked the brush, and my lips got all red!" Scientific thinking is based on observing, testing, and evaluating outcomes. Preschoolers constantly do a less-formalized version.

Conservation: Knowing that the arrangement of things can be changed while their amount remains the same. Count out two groups of ten paper clips. Pile one up, and stretch the other into a line. Which one has more? Kids who haven't yet grasped this new concept will tell you that the line has more (because it looks like more). By the age of eight, children understand that arrangement and quantity are separate ideas.

Correspondence: Learning that, for example, the number one represents one thing. "One sticker, please. No, I meant two."

Counting: Knowing the names of the numbers in order. "Look at all those fish. Let's count how many you drew. One, two, . . ."

Creativity (also called imagination): Combining elements in different ways to achieve a new result. "Sam made a man out of peas and carrots." "I like to paint with a spoon—it's fun."

Fine Motor Coordination: Developing hand-and-finger dexterity and strength, as well as hand-eye coordination.

Matching: Identifying alike and not alike. "Jana, are these two colors the same?" "How are those dogs different?" "Can you draw another eye just the same?"

Measuring: Learning to compare. "Is your sister bigger than you?" "Hand me the biggest paper, please." Later, kids learn to use a unit to measure. "The phone is three steps away." Eventually, children master measuring with a standard unit of measure such as feet and inches.

Ordering: Learning to put things in the order of a particular quality, such as color, size, or time. Understanding dark to light, tall to short, or big to small. "Look, you made big, medium, and little balls of clay."

Patterning: Learning to recognize and create patterns. "Blue, red, blue, red, . . . What color bead comes next?" Patterns can be visual, verbal, musical, numerical, or kinetic—anything at all.

Planning: Thinking about how to achieve a particular result. "Big teeth will make the monster scary." "More bricks for a bigger tower!"

Predicting: Observing and guessing what comes next. "Sam, what do you think will happen if we put this crayon in the oven?"

Problem Solving: Coming up with solutions to situations that demand an answer. "How can I make these stick?" Intelligence has been defined as knowing what to do when you don't know what to do.

Reversibility: Understanding that some processes can be "undone" (such as molding a lump of clay), and some can't (such as baking cookies).

Sorting and Classifying: Learning to group things by their properties. Children begin sorting by using one property. "All the yellow ones go in the can." As their skill becomes more advanced, they can sort by using more than one characteristic. "Red bumpy ones go together, and the other red ones go there."

Symbolic Representation: Using marks or objects to represent a thing or an idea. "Look! Two raisins make eyes." "To make a snake, I drew a long, squiggly line."

Vocabulary: Learning how to express ideas is as important as knowing the names for things. Talking with your child about his art offers an opportunity for meaningful conversation as well as learning new words.

★ INDEX ★

Use this index to quickly find an appropriate activity for wherever you happen to be. Check the Contents at the front of this book for a complete activity list.

$8.95 FPT

$11.95 in Canada

Razzle Dazzle Doodle **Art**

Little kids love color, the feel of fur, and the crinkle of foil. They like making marks, experimenting with tape or glue, and finding shapes and patterns. They're natural artists who love the process, and they're at the magical age when they're seldom disappointed by their results.

But . . . who has the time to get out all the stuff and then clean up the mess?

Relax. This book is full of projects—some as neat as a pile of paper clips, some as quiet as lying on a grassy hill and looking at clouds, and others as wild and crazy as painting naked in the bathtub (with special do-it-yourself soap colors).

Inside this book you'll find art suitable for the backseat of the car, the doctor's waiting room, and the kitchen sink. You already have most of the materials. And many of the projects take very little grown-up help.

Art is where your child will explore hands-on creativity, learn the meaning of marks and symbols, discover how parts and patterns fit together, and experiment with cause and effect. And it's a razzle dazzle doodle way to just plain fun.

09940870

Linda Allison and Martha Weston are no strangers to kids. Since 1975, they have produced such Brown Paper School favorites as *Blood and Guts*; *Gee, Wiz!*; *The I Hate Mathematics! Book*; and *The Book of Think*. With other Brown Paper School authors, they have influenced a generation of American children.

Now they have turned their attention to a second generation. The results are *Eenie Meenie Miney Math!*; *Wordsaroni*; *Razzle Dazzle Doodle Art*; and *Pint-Size Science*—the first four books in the new Brown Paper Preschool series.

Linda mostly writes. And Martha mostly draws. They test their ideas on many parents, children, and teachers. The results are in this book.

The authors work in a sunny shingled studio just north of San Francisco. Between them they have two devoted husbands, three kids, a few pets, and many thousands of friends in and out of the classroom.

Printed in Hong Kong